LEADERS OF THE
MIDDLE AGES™

CHARLEMAGNE The Life and
Times of an Early
Medieval Emperor

LEADERS OF THE
MIDDLE AGES™

CHARLEMAGNE

The Life and
Times of an Early
Medieval Emperor

Tehmina Bhote

The Rosen Publishing Group, Inc., New York

To all young students of history, may you be inspired by the past

Published in 2005 by The Rosen Publishing Group, Inc.
29 East 21st Street, New York, NY 10010

First Edition

Library of Congress Cataloging-in-Publication Data

Bhote, Tehmina.
Charlemagne : the life and times of an early medieval emperor / by Tehmina Bhote.
    p. cm. — (Leaders of the Middle Ages)
Includes bibliographical references and index.
ISBN 1-4042-0161-0 (library binding)
1. Charlemagne, Emperor, 742–814. 2. France—Kings and rulers—
Biography. 3. Holy Roman Empire—Kings and rulers—Biography.
4. France—History—To 987. 5. Holy Roman Empire—History—To 1517.
[1. Charlemagne, Emperor, 742–814. 2. Kings, queens, rulers, etc.
3. Holy Roman Empire—History—To 1517. 4. Civilization, Medieval.]
I. Title. II. Series.
DC73.B42 2004
944'.0142'092—dc22

                                                    2003023748

Manufactured in the United States of America

On the cover: Inset: Reliquary bust of Charlemagne donated in 1349 by Karl IV. Top: Charlemagne sends ambassadors out to his empire. Bottom: Coronation of Charlemagne by Pope Leo III, from a French illuminated manuscript, 1450.

CONTENTS

LAND AT THE TIME OF CHARLEMAGNE

● Paderborn

Aachen ●

● Mainz

● Paris

River Loire

● Poitiers

ALPS

● Pavia

Basque area

Battle of
Roncesvalles
●

PYRENEES

● Rome

Pamplona

Barcelona ●

MEDITERRANEAN SEA

AFRICA

INTRODUCTION: FATHER OF EUROPE

Charlemagne (pronounced SHAR-la-mane) was a German king, as well as the emperor of most of western Europe. He lived more than 1,200 years ago, between 742 and 814. He is one of the most famous and powerful leaders ever to have ruled in Europe. In fact, some historians have called him the father of Europe.

According to evidence from historical documents written both while he was emperor and hundreds of years afterward, Charlemagne was a great leader and warrior. He was a fair man, but he could also be ruthless. He made many laws to keep order in society, and he encouraged learning. During his reign, many churches and palaces were built, some of which are still standing. Charlemagne's goal was to unite western Europe the way it had been during the time of the ancient Roman Empire.

There is no evidence to suggest where Charlemagne was born. It is likely, though, that it was somewhere in modern-day Germany. It's possible that he was, in fact, born in the town of Aachen, where he later spent most of his life. Charlemagne came from the German Arnulfing family. They spoke a language similar to today's German. His father was Pepin the Short, and his mother was called Bertrada.

During Charlemagne's life, he was called Charles (or Karl in German) by his family and his court. He would also have been known as Charles by his subjects and other rulers. More than 300 years after his death, he was made a saint. Then people began to call him Charlemagne, which means "Charles the Great" in French. In German, he is called Karl der Grosse which also means "Charles the Great."

Charlemagne was a Frank. The Franks were a German tribe who controlled the area of northwest-ern Europe that is now northern France and western Germany. They gained a lot of power in early medieval times after the Roman Empire in western Europe crumbled. Frankish leaders had been ruling much of Europe for hundreds of years before Charlemagne. However, Charlemagne built an even bigger empire during his forty-seven-year reign.

This is a fourteenth-century reliquary bust of Charlemagne. Reliquaries were containers in shrines that were used for storing different parts of a saint's body. This reliquary contains Charlemagne's skull. It was believed that the relics (either parts of the body or items associated with the saint, such as clothing) possessed power—especially healing powers. Because of this, relics were often spread over a wide area. Pilgrims would touch or kiss the relics, hoping to receive their healing powers. This bust was donated to the Cathedral Treasury at Aachen in 1349 by the Holy Roman Emperor Charles IV.

By the time of his death in 814, Charlemagne had expanded his empire from modern-day France, Belgium, and the Netherlands to include Germany, Luxembourg, Switzerland, Austria, northern Spain, and northern Italy. In early medieval times, European countries or kingdoms were known by different names. The kingdom Charlemagne came from was called Austrasia, which is now in Germany.

The center of Charlemagne's empire was Aachen. Aachen is a city in western Germany near modern-day Belgium. It was here that he built his palace and a remarkable church. The church is one of the most important historic buildings in the world. It is a rare example of early medieval architecture from western Europe. It survived many wars, including World War II (1939–1945).

His palace also housed a school. Charlemagne's Palace School was built for both monks and lay-people (those who are not members of the clergy). Charlemagne sent for some of the best teachers in Europe for his school. The emperor was passionate about education. He thought it was important that people in his empire have the opportunity to learn how to read, especially the Bible. Charlemagne was one of the first rulers in Europe to support good education for his subjects. Many other schools were created in his empire.

Charlemagne was a Christian ruler who was anointed as an emperor by the pope on Christmas Day in the year 800. He was an ally (or friend) of the pope in Rome throughout his reign. Charlemagne defended the pope against other leaders who threatened the pope and his lands. Charlemagne was also passionate about being a good Christian ruler. Often, when he defeated pagan tribes such as the Saxons, he gave them the choice of baptism or death.

By the time Charlemagne died at the age of seventy-two, his Frankish Empire was as big as the Byzantine Empire. In fact, it had become the largest empire in Europe since that of the ancient Romans. No European leader has ruled over so much of Europe since. In 1165, Charlemagne was made a saint by one of his successors, during the reign of Emperor Frederick Barbarossa.

How
CHARLEMAGNE
CAME TO POWER

Charlemagne ruled during the early Middle Ages (about 500 to 1000). The time between the end of the ancient Roman Empire in western Europe and the reign of Charlemagne is often called the Dark Ages. This is because we have little existing information about what life was like in this period. In contrast, many documents have survived from the ancient Greeks and Romans.

However, it is known that many buildings and cities continued to be built in Europe and people still traded with each other. Similar to today, early medieval Europe, was a place where many different races of people lived. These races, known as tribes, were groups of people who shared a similar language and culture. The tribes exchanged customs and ideas. They also had their own styles of clothing. Some also used different types of weapons and had different ways of fighting battles.

This is a detail from a floor mosaic from ancient Rome, dated to the third century. The mosaic, which was part of a series or cycle of the months of the year, depicts two men stepping on grapes to extract the juice for winemaking. This particular mosaic illustrates the month of September. The art of winemaking was an important Roman industry. Wine was exported across the empire. With the fall of the Roman Empire, much knowledge was lost. Nonetheless, winemaking continued, and German and French wines are part of this inheritance.

MEDIEVAL RELIGION

Since the time of the first Christian Roman emperor, Constantine (272–337), Christians in Europe were able to build their own churches and worship freely after their persecution by the Romans ended around 330. When the Roman

From the Church of San Vitale in Ravenna, Italy, this mosaic shows Byzantine emperor Justinian I. The mosaic dates from before 547. It is an example of Byzantine figurative art, a style that was at its height during Charlemagne's reign. The emperor (center) *is wearing a dark cloak, and Archbishop Maximian* (standing next to him) *is holding a cross. Ravenna was the capital of the Byzantine territories in Italy until 751, when it was captured by the Lombards.*

Empire split in two during Constantine's reign, the church also split into the Catholic Church and the Eastern Orthodox Church.

During Charlemagne's reign, the way the two churches worshipped was similar. The main difference was language. Catholics used Latin in their ceremonies and to write their books. Meanwhile, the Eastern Orthodox Church used Greek. The pope in Rome was the leader of the Catholic Church. The patriarch of Constantinople (present-day Istanbul) was the leader of the Eastern Orthodox Church. The patriarch crowned the Byzantine emperor, who was called the basileus in Greek. Many people still practiced their own native (pagan) religions. There were also many Muslims living in southern Europe. They mainly resided in what are now Spain, Portugal, and Sicily. Communities of Jews lived all across Europe.

MAJOR POWERS IN EUROPE BEFORE CHARLEMAGNE

In the year 476, the ancient Romans finally lost control of the capital, Rome, and their empire in western Europe. In the last years of the Roman Empire in western Europe, many different tribes that had lived both inside and outside the Roman

Empire began to conquer and rule western Europe for themselves. In the sixth and seventh centuries, a German tribe called the Lombards invaded and settled in northern Italy. The city of Pavia, where they built a royal palace, became the center of their new kingdom.

Before Charlemagne, the most powerful rulers in Europe were the Byzantine emperors. The Byzantine Empire, also known as the Eastern Roman Empire, covered southeastern Europe. It included parts of western Asia (Asia Minor) to modern-day Greece, southern Italy, and parts of eastern Europe such as Yugoslavia and the Balkans.

The empire was created around the year 330 by the Roman emperor Constantine. He had moved the capital city from Rome in the west to Constantinople in the east. During the fourth to sixth centuries, the Byzantines fought many wars against the German tribes of Europe, the Persian Empire, and Muslim rulers.

The Byzantines believed they were the heirs of the ancient Roman Empire. Even many of the other European leaders considered the Byzantine emperors to be the most superior and important leaders in Europe. They were Christian and followed Roman law and customs. However, the official language of their empire was Greek. Latin was the official language of western Europe. By the time Charlemagne came to power in the year 768 (when his father, the Frankish king Pepin the Short, died), the Byzantines had the wealthiest empire in the known world. This was because they were at the heart of all the important trade routes between the east and the west. Their art and buildings mixed styles from Persia and the east with Roman styles from the west. This architectural mix was greatly admired by Charlemagne.

From the sixth to the eighth centuries, the island of Britain and the far north of Europe (Scandinavia) were invaded by different tribes. The tribes, such as the Angles, Saxons, and Jutes, made their kingdoms in these places after the Romans lost power.

By the eighth century, Muslim leaders ruled over land in what are now southern and central Spain and parts of southern Italy. Muslim kings were called emirs or caliphs. The Muslim rulers remained there for the next 500 years. However, there were still some small Christian kingdoms in northern Spain. As well, the Basque tribe controlled the Marches, or borders along the vast mountain range of the Pyrenees. Charlemagne never ruled over Britain, Scandinavia, southern Spain, or southern Italy.

This is an illustration from a manual, dated around 1050, that indicates which days are high days and which are holy days in the church calendar. In the image, a man is encouraging his oxen to plow the fields. The plowman has to hold down the plow so that it makes a deep line, or furrow, in the ground. Beside him, another man is scattering seeds. During Charlemagne's time, the Franks and the rest of the European tribes were agrarian workers, meaning that they worked the land.

THE FRANKS: CHARLEMAGNE'S TRIBE

Charlemagne's tribe, the Franks, came from Belgium, northeastern France, and parts of western Germany. The Franks, whose language was similar to modern German, were very important in the history of early medieval Europe. They were probably the most successful German tribe that built its own kingdom

after the fall of the Romans in western Europe. And they were able to keep control of it. Most Franks lived in the countryside in small villages rather than in big towns and cities. Local nobles acted like small kings in different parts of the kingdom.

In the fourth and fifth centuries, the Franks were both Christians and pagans. King Merovech was one of the first famous Frankish leaders. He gave his name to the Merovingian dynasty. This was the family line from which the Franks elected their kings. The most powerful nobles in the kingdom chose the future kings.

In the year 481, Clovis became king of the Franks when he was only fifteen years old. He fought many wars, defeated other tribes that were ruling small kingdoms in Gaul (France), and brought their lands into the Frankish kingdom. Clovis was a pagan king, but his wife, Clotilda, was a Christian. According to one legend, during a fierce war with the Alemanni tribe (another German tribe) in the year 496, Clovis prayed to the god his wife worshipped, promising to become a Christian if he won. He did win, and he was baptized on Christmas Day along with many members of his army. Clovis became the first Christian king of the Franks. The later Frankish kings were also Christian.

THE FRANKS RISE TO POWER

By the seventh century, the Merovingian kings were losing their power to influential Frankish warrior-nobles. These nobles owned many lands in the Frankish kingdom. They also led armies into war with other rulers. By the early eighth century, the mayors of the palace (the nobles) were actually running the kingdom in place of the king.

Charles Martel, Charlemagne's grandfather, became a mayor of the palace. In the year 732, Charles led an army to the city of Poitiers in Gaul to fight against the Muslim army that was advancing into northern Europe from Spain. Charles was successful and defeated the Muslim leader Abd al-Rahman. The Muslim rulers were never again able to invade farther into Europe.

Pepin the Short, Charlemagne's father, was also one of the mayors for the Merovingian kings. Pepin was from the Arnulfing family. He and his wife, Bertrada, had two sons, Charles (Charlemagne) and

EINHARD AND THE *VITA CAROLI*

A Frankish monk named Einhard wrote an important chronicle called, in Latin, *Vita Caroli* (Life of Charles). Einhard wrote the *Vita Caroli* in about 830, shortly after the emperor died. Einhard was a close friend and trusted adviser of Charlemagne. He witnessed the events and people he describes in the *Vita Caroli*. Einhard wrote much of his story from memory and from the notes he made about the events he attended and people he knew during Charlemagne's reign. Because Einhard was such a great friend of Charlemagne's, his story does not describe many of the bad points about the emperor and his reign. However, Einhard's book is the most accurate existing documentation of Charlemagne's reign.

The *Vita Caroli* gives a lot of important information about Charlemagne's wars, his family life, his pastimes, the palaces and churches he had built, and how he died. In the book, Einhard explains the reason why he was the right person to write the *Vita Caroli*:

> I am very conscious of the fact that no
> one can describe these events more

> accurately than I, for I was present when they took place and, as they say, I saw them with my own eyes.
>
> Einhard also felt that no one else would write about Charlemagne. In fact, Charlemagne has been written about by more authors than any other ruler of early medieval Europe.

Carloman. Carloman was many years younger than Charlemagne. The Arnulfings later became known as the Carolingians. Einhard said he could not write anything about Charlemagne's childhood in *Vita Caroli*. As he notes,

> I consider that it would be foolish of me to write about Charlemagne's birth and child-hood, or even about his boyhood, for nothing is set down in writing about this and nobody can be found still alive who claims to have any personal knowledge of these matters.

However, it is likely that Charlemagne and his brother, Carloman, were brought up to learn how to hunt, fight, and ride horses like other Frankish men. They would also have learned about running a kingdom from their father, Pepin.

Pepin himself was elected king by the Frankish nobles in the year 751. At the time, Charlemagne was about nine years old. This was the start of the Carolingian dynasty. In the same year, Pepin had his coronation at the Abbey of Saint Denis, just outside Paris, France. The previous Frankish kings had been buried at the abbey. Pepin was anointed with oil by Bishop Boniface, an Anglo-Saxon monk from Britain. Charlemagne's mother was also crowned and anointed—in fact, she was the first Frankish queen to be crowned in the same way as the king.

PEPIN AND CHARLEMAGNE HELP THE POPE

Also in 751, Pope Stephen II, who was the most powerful bishop and religious leader in Europe, was threatened by the Lombard king Aistulf. Aistulf wanted the pope and the city of Rome to come under his rule. The Lombard kingdom already covered most of northern and southern Italy. A small strip of land in central Italy (which included Rome) belonged to the Byzantine emperors. Until 751, the popes had relied on the Byzantine emperors for help in difficult times. But the Byzantine emperors were fighting other wars and could not come to the pope's aid.

Two years later, in 753, Pope Stephen II traveled from Rome to the Frankish kingdom. He had already approved of Pepin as the new king. In fact, Pope Stephen II wanted Pepin and the Franks to be his allies in his fight against the Lombards. Pepin thought the support of the pope would legitimize his rule.

The Imperial Annals were official records written about the Frankish rulers and their activities. It is in these annals that Charlemagne first appears on written record. The annals say that, at age eleven, Charlemagne was sent to meet the pope upon his arrival in the Frankish kingdom. This was an exciting time for the Franks because no pope had ever visited the Frankish kingdom. Because the Arnulfings were devout Catholic Christians, the approval of the pope was especially important to them.

In the summer of 754, Pope Stephen II repeated the coronation of Pepin and Bertrada. This time, Pepin's sons, Charlemagne and Carloman, were also anointed as kings by the pope. The pope also gave Pepin and his sons the important titles of protectors of Rome. By doing so, the pope hoped he would be able to ask the Frankish kings for help if he were being attacked by other leaders in Europe.

That same year, Pepin raised an army to go to Italy and fight against King Aistulf and the Lombards,

In this fourteenth-century French manuscript, Charlemagne is leading his army in a battle charge. The manuscript this illustration is from is called *Entrée d'Espagne* (Entry of Spain). The image may be referring to Charlemagne's wars in Spain and the Battle of Roncesvalles.

thereby honoring his promise to the pope. Pepin's army crossed the Alps from modern-day France and fought against the Lombards. Charlemagne, who was twelve at the time, probably rode over the Alps with his father into the war.

Even though the Frankish army was smaller, it won and King Aistulf was defeated. Pepin took mercy on the king and spared him his life. However, in the year 756, Pepin and the Franks had to fight against the Lombards again. It is almost certain that Charlemagne went to Italy during this campaign against the Lombards. It was expected that, at the age of fourteen, Frankish boys became men and were old enough to fight. Finally, the Lombards were defeated. They agreed upon terms of peace with the pope and the Franks.

In a famous act—the Donation of Pepin—Pepin gave the old lands in central Italy that belonged to the Byzantine emperors to Pope Stephen II. These lands were known as the Papal States. A small part of the Papal States still exists today. This is the Vatican City in Rome. It is owned by the pope himself. Throughout Charlemagne's reign, he would remain a close ally of the popes in Rome.

CHARLEMAGNE BECOMES KING OF THE FRANKS

For the rest of Pepin's reign, Charlemagne was a commander in the Frankish army. The army mainly fought against the Duke of Aquitaine who ruled over the region of southwestern Gaul (France) from the Loire River to the Pyrenees mountains. Because there was fertile farming land, many cities, and good trade, this was a wealthy area in Europe during the early Middle Ages. After nine years and many long campaigns, Pepin won over Aquitaine and added this important area to his Frankish kingdom.

However, in the year 768, shortly after his campaigns in Aquitaine had ended, Pepin became ill with a fever. He knew he would not live long. Accordingly, he divided his kingdom into two, which was the tradition of the Franks. One part was given to Charlemagne (the northern and western areas), the other to Carloman (the southern and eastern areas). After Pepin died, Charlemagne, Carloman, and Bertrada traveled with his body to the Abbey of Saint Denis, where Pepin was buried.

Charlemagne and Carloman became joint rulers of the Frankish kingdom. This covered almost all of present-day France, Belgium, the Netherlands, Germany, Switzerland, Austria, and Luxembourg. In October 768, when Charlemagne was twenty-six, he and his brother were crowned kings of the Franks in their own parts of the kingdom.

As a result, many of the influential Frankish nobles plotted against Charlemagne and Carloman. They tried to persuade them to fight each other so the nobles could gain more power for themselves. But the plots did not work. This was mainly because their mother, Bertrada, used her influence to keep the peace between the two brothers. However, after a few years, Carloman died. Because Carloman's two sons were too young to rule, Charlemagne took over his brother's half of the Frankish kingdom. In the year 771, Charlemagne was elected king of the Franks.

THE PRIVATE LIFE OF AN EMPEROR

CHAPTER 2

1

3

4

5

6

7

Charlemagne had four wives (it was not unusual for early medieval rulers to marry more than once), and he was the father of about eighteen children. However, only eight were the children of his wives. The others were children of his mistresses, who were women in his court.

It is probable that before Charlemagne was made king in 768 he lived with, but did not officially marry, a woman called Himiltrude. It is thought that he and Himiltrude had a disabled son called Pepin the Hunchback. Because he was disabled, the Franks believed he should not become king or have an official role in Charlemagne's kingdom. He died in 810 or 811.

Charlemagne's first official wife was the daughter of the Lombard king Desiderius. They were married around 770. Some historians believe she was

This is a page from a manuscript containing the text of *Vita Caroli* (Life of Charles). It was written by a monk named Einhard around 830, sixteen years after Charlemagne's death in 814. It is believed that this manuscript is the most accurate account of Charlemagne's life and times.

called Desiderata. Medieval rulers often married into powerful families to keep peace between kingdoms. Charlemagne's first marriage may have been arranged by Pepin after he made peace with the Lombards. Einhard writes in the *Vita Caroli*: "Nobody knows why, but he [Charlemagne] dismissed this wife after one year."

If an early medieval ruler no longer wished to be married to his wife, the king or emperor was allowed to marry another woman without having to get a divorce. In later medieval times, the Catholic Church made laws that required a ruler to ask the permission of the pope before ending a marriage.

Charlemagne's second wife, Hildigard, was from a noble family of the German Swabian tribe. She was the mother of Charlemagne's three most-famous sons—Charles, Pepin, and Louis (later called Louis the Pious). It was Louis who inherited Charlemagne's empire after his father's death. Hildigard died in the year 783.

Charlemagne's third wife, Fastrada, was a Frank. She was blamed by many nobles for plotting twice to kill Charlemagne. It was also thought that she was a bad influence on Charlemagne. According to Einhard in the *Vita Caroli*,

> The cruelty of Queen Fastrada is thought to have been the cause of both these conspiracies, since it was under her influence that Charlemagne seemed to have taken actions that were fundamentally opposed to his normal kindliness and good nature.

Fastrada died in the year 794. Charlemagne's last wife, Liutgard, was a noblewoman from the Alamanni tribe. They did not have any children together. Liutgard died in the year 800. During the last fourteen years of his life, Charlemagne did not remarry.

This sapphire in an ornate gold setting is said to have been Charlemagne's talisman (a good luck charm). The sapphire is surrounded by pearls and other precious stones.

FAMILY MAN

Charlemagne enjoyed the company of his children and took a great interest in both his sons and daughters. He always preferred his family to travel with him, just like he had done with his father, Pepin.

A monk from Charlemagne's court named Theodulf once wrote a poem describing a scene in Charlemagne's family. He noted that Charlemagne's children gathered around him when he came home. His sons would take off his cloak and sword, and his six daughters would give him hugs and bring him bread, wine, apples, and flowers.

Then, the bishop would come and bless the food of Charlemagne and his family. According to the poem, Charlemagne was so fond of his daughters that he could not bear to be without them. Because of this, they stayed with Charlemagne and did not get married.

Though they remained unmarried, they had many children. Some of the fathers of their children were men who fought against each other to be the Frankish ruler after Charlemagne died in 814. Charlemagne's mother, Bertrada, also lived with him until her death in the year 783. This was the same year as the death of his second wife, Hildigard. Einhard noted that he loved Bertrada very much and when she died, he "buried her with great honor in the Church of Saint Denis, where his father lay."

LOOKING LIKE AN EMPEROR

The *Vita Caroli* also describes what Charlemagne looked like. On important occasions, such as meetings with foreign ambassadors or grand feasts, he would wear embroidered robes (probably silk), a golden brooch, shoes with jewels, and a crown. Similar to Byzantine rulers, Charlemagne had his visitors lie flat on the ground at his feet to greet him. Charlemagne also admired the royal ceremonies of the Byzantine rulers.

Charlemagne's preferred clothing was his everyday attire: a linen shirt; short, tight trousers (called breeches); a woolen tunic; and leather shoes. He also carried a sword. These were the normal clothes of Frankish nobles. In the winter, he sometimes wore a

coat made of otter skins. Einhard writes, "He hated the clothes of foreign countries, no matter how becoming they might be, and he would never [agree] to wearing them."

Other chronicles describe Charlemagne as a very tall man with blond hair, a long nose, and a moustache but no beard. Since the Frankish leaders usually had long hair, Charlemagne would almost certainly have had long hair too.

LIFE AT HOME

Einhard also wrote that Charlemagne did not like drinking too much, and he hated people who got very drunk. However, he did like to eat and he enjoyed his food. He complained that fasting made him feel sick. Charlemagne's favorite food was roast meat. He

This is an eighth- or ninth-century manuscript illustration of Charlemagne and one of his wives (it is not known which one). In the image, the king of the Franks is wearing cross-gartered breeches. This means that the garters—usually used to hold up stockings—were wrapped crosswise around the leg of the breeches to hold the fabric tightly to the leg. It was more practical to have the fabric close to the leg when riding a horse. The garters would also show off the different colors of the breeches.

This fourteenth-century Italian painting of a royal banquet illustrates what went on during similar feasts and banquets during Charlemagne's time. The atmosphere is very festive. Musicians are playing and servants are preparing a lavish meal.

enjoyed meat such as venison and wild boar that was brought home from hunts. While eating (with members of his family, people of his court, or by himself), he would listen to old stories about ancient heroes.

On important occasions and religious festivals, he put on feasts and banquets. At these grand events, many guests would be invited and musicians, dancers, and singers provided the entertainment. Musicians played instruments such as simple flutes, small drums, rattles, and stringed instruments, which were plucked. Banquets were also put on when important people—such as foreign rulers and ambassadors—came to visit the emperor and for occasions such as weddings. Charlemagne himself had four grand banquets for his four weddings. Large feasts and banquets were like long festivals and could last for a whole week.

Charlemagne was a light sleeper, and he would get up many times during the night. Sometimes, he spent all day in his bedchamber. If he was asked to solve a problem, such as what to do about disobedient laborers on the royal estate or a quarrel between members of his court, he would often summon all the people involved to his bedchamber and give his orders from there.

Charlemagne enjoyed reading, especially Christian books. His favorite pastimes were horseback riding and hunting. The Franks were well known for their skills in both these activities. Charlemagne also liked swimming. Einhard stated, "He was an extremely strong swimmer and in this sport, no one could surpass [beat] him." In addition to these pastimes, Charlemagne liked to bathe in the natural hot springs of Aachen with his family and friends.

MEDIEVAL EVIDENCE

Like Einhard, medieval monks wrote about Charlemagne's life in what are known as chronicles. Songs or poems called chansons (French for "songs") also provide evidence concerning the details of Charlemagne's life and what people in later medieval times thought of him.

Many medieval chronicles were written hundreds of years after the actual events took place. Aside from Einhard's *Vita Caroli*, there is another famous chronicle about Charlemagne. This one was written by a monk named Notker the Stammerer who was in the Saint Gall monastery in Switzerland. Written in about 884, the Latin *De Carolo Magno*, which means "About Charles the Great," appeared eighty years after Charlemagne's death.

Notker the Stammerer would not have met Charlemagne. It is likely that he was asked to write this chronicle for Charlemagne's son Louis the Pious. The people writing these stories obtained their information from various sources, including stories passed down through oral tradition, manuscripts such as annals, official records such as laws, and people's letters. Some of these documents still survive.

Some of the information historians have learned about Charlemagne's physical appearance is based on statues of him. One of the most well-known statues of the emperor is a bust (head, shoulders, and chest) made of gold, silver, and precious gems that actually contains Charlemagne's skull. (His body was dug up in 1349, and his skull was placed in this reliquary bust.)

The bust was made in 1349 under the orders of Emperor Charles IV, who was one of Charlemagne's successors. It is kept in the treasury of Aachen Cathedral in Germany. There are also many

There is some debate surrounding this bronze statuette (called an equestrian statuette). While most historians believe that the man shown is Charlemagne, others think it may actually be his grandson, Charles the Bald. One of the reasons for this uncertainty is that the dating of the statuette is unclear. It is not certain whether it was cast in Aachen (also known as Aix-la-Chapelle) in the early ninth century (which makes it most likely to be a statuette of Charlemagne) or later in the ninth century. The statuette measures 9.4 inches (24 centimeters) in height.

other statues of Charlemagne across Europe. Some were made during his life, while others were created many years later. A bronze statue housed in the Louvre Museum in Paris features Charlemagne on his horse.

Other images of Charlemagne were created on illuminated manuscripts. These were all painted after he died. Monks painted these images on the manuscripts they wrote and copied by hand. There were also coins featuring images of Charlemagne. Though few buildings from Charlemagne's time have survived, archaeologists have dug up many ruins that indicate what type of places people lived in back then.

As well, artifacts such as jewelry, pots, tools, and coins provide insight into life during Charlemagne's reign. All this provides historians and archaeologists with evidence of the type of things the merchants in Charlemagne's empire traded. For example, food and drink left in pots indicates what people ate and drank. And remains of animal bones show what type of animals medieval people ate.

FROM KINGDOM TO EMPIRE

Because he wanted to create an even bigger empire, Charlemagne was nearly always at war. He mainly fought against other German tribes. All in all, Charlemagne waged fifty-three wars, many of which he led himself. Some of the wars, like the ones against the Saxons, lasted for most of his reign.

Soon after Charlemagne became the sole king of the Franks in 771, he set about continuing his father's work in expanding the Frankish kingdom. Charlemagne and his army continued a war against the nobles in Aquitaine that had been started by Carloman; he eventually won. Hunold, Duke of Aquitaine, surrendered as did Lupus, the Duke of Gascony, who was an ally of Hunold. Both Aquitaine and Gascony were then incorporated into Charlemagne's kingdom, which covered most of the area of present-day France.

CHARLEMAGNE'S ARMY

In Charlemagne's army, Frankish nobles acted as generals. Under Frankish law, many of these nobles were expected to join the military. The nobles also had to recruit and train foot soldiers (infantry) and good horsemen (cavalry). Some of these warriors were mercenaries, whose full-time job was fighting wars. Many other soldiers were serfs or peasants who worked on a noble's land. They had to fight if they were asked to by their local noble. If they did not, they would suf-

fer a penalty such as being thrown off the noble's land and losing their job as a farmer or laborer.

This image is from a French illuminated manuscript called Les Grandes Chroniques de France *(The Great Chronicles of France). The illustration shows Charlemagne receiving messengers. They have come to tell him the news of the victory against the Saracens. Western Europeans called Muslims "Saracens"; the term was most commonly used during the Crusades.*

Charlemagne's armies were constantly fighting to defend the empire. As a reward, Charlemagne gave the army leaders estates to live on where they could earn money from the serfs and peasants who worked on the land. This meant that Charlemagne's commanders were loyal to him and were always willing to fight for him.

Charlemagne's navy was set up to defend his empire against the "Northmen," or Vikings. He had a large fleet of ships built to patrol major rivers in the empire such as the Rhine and the Meuse. He also had guard towers built in all the port towns and at the mouths of rivers. This way it would be possible to keep watch for any attacks. Other rulers were not as good at creating sea and river defenses.

CHARLEMAGNE BECOMES KING OF THE LOMBARDS

Charlemagne had married his first wife, the daughter of the Lombard king Desiderius, in about 770. He left her just a year later, which supposedly made Desiderius very angry. The marriage should have guaranteed a peace between the Franks and the Lombards. Shortly after 771, Desiderius began to attack Rome and Pope Adrian I, who was Stephen III's successor. Desiderius seized the pope and his residence, Saint Peter's Palace. Adrian sent a messenger to Charlemagne with a plea to come to his aid against the Lombards. He reminded Charlemagne that he was protector of Rome and had a duty to help the pope.

By the spring of 773, negotiations with Desiderius had failed. Charlemagne mobilized his army and started the march from Thionville in Gaul over the Alps to Rome. The army arrived in northern Italy via two routes so that they could surround Desiderius's forces.

Leading from the front, Charlemagne commanded the army in person. By September, he had captured many of the Lombard cities. Some local nobles joined Charlemagne's forces. When he reached Pavia, the capital city of Lombard, he surrounded the walls with his army and began a siege.

This meant that no supplies could enter Pavia. Representatives of the pope came to greet Charlemagne and hail him as their savior and emperor. In June 774, Pavia surrendered to Charlemagne and Desiderius was exiled. In the same year, Charlemagne became king of the Lombards.

THE SAXON WARS

Charlemagne's longest, most expensive, and fiercest wars were against the Saxons. The Saxons were a threat to the Frankish Empire, and Charlemagne was determined to defeat them and bring them into his empire. The Saxons were also pagans (heathens), and Charlemagne wanted to convert the Saxon tribe to Christianity.

As Einhard describes the Saxons in *Vita Caroli*, "No war ever undertaken by the Frankish people was more prolonged, more full of atrocities [terrible things] or more demanding of effort. The Saxons, like almost all the peoples living in Germany, are ferocious by nature."

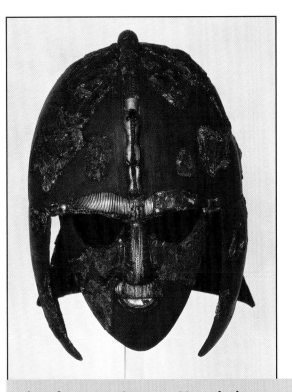

The famous Sutton Hoo helmet dates from the seventh century. This iron helmet with gold and silver decorations was worn by Saxons in battle. The helmet was excavated from a burial site in East Anglia, England. Various parts of the helmet were found during excavations in 1939. The helmet was reconstructed in 1947 and again in 1970. It is looked after by the British Museum in London, where it is on display.

In the year 772, Charlemagne destroyed a sacred pagan symbol called Irminsul. This was a giant carved pillar near a temple in the town of Marseburg in modern-day northeastern Germany. Although Charlemagne was generally merciful to his enemies, he could also inflict terrible punishments on them. In the year 782, he ordered the executions of more than 4,500 unarmed Saxons. In 785, he decided to try and end the war peacefully by asking Widukind, the Saxon leader, to become a Christian. Widukind agreed for the sake of peace. After this, many more Saxons were baptized.

THE BATTLE OF RONCESVALLES

In the year 777, the Muslim emirs of Spain traveled to Paderborn to ask Charlemagne for assistance against the Christian Basque tribe in northern Spain. Paderborn was one of Charlemagne's royal palaces. They promised to give their own army in support of the invasion. However, when Charlemagne and his army invaded the Basque territories in 778, no help arrived from the Muslim rulers. Although Charlemagne's army fought hard and destroyed the Basque cities of Pamplona and Barcelona, they were finally defeated at the Battle of Roncesvalles. The

LA CHANSON DE ROLAND

Written almost 400 years after his death, *La Chanson de Roland*, or "The Song of Roland," is the most famous song ever written about Charlemagne's times. It was written in Old French in about 1150. It is a *chanson de geste*, or a "song of deeds." This means that a storyteller would recite the song to an audience who would follow each episode carefully and wait anxiously to find out the end of the story.

It is not known who wrote the chanson. It is interesting to compare *La Chanson de Roland* (based on the story of one of Charlemagne's battles in northern Spain) to what Einhard wrote in *Vita Caroli*. This is because historians know that Einhard's version of events is more accurate. The first verse of the chanson is worded as follows:

> Charles the king, our Lord and Sovereign,
>
> Full seven years hath [has] sojourned [journied] in Spain,
>
> Conquered the land, and won the western main,
>
> Now no fortress against him doth [does] remain.

This is a detail from a relief depicting warriors in a scene from the Battle of Roncesvalles, which is written about in La Chanson de Roland. *The battle took place in 777 and 778. This relief is part of the Saint Pierre Cathedral in the French city of Angoulême. Construction of the cathedral started in 1101 and was completed in 1130.*

According to *Vita Caroli*, the Battle of Roncesvalles in northern Spain took place during the years 777 and 778, when Charlemagne was thirty-six years old. Roland, a French noble from Charlemagne's army, was killed along with some other nobles during the battle that

Charlemagne lost against the Christian Basque tribe from the Pyrenees mountains in northern Spain. In *La Chanson de Roland*, Roland is described as one of Charlemagne's nephews. He is the hero of the battle and one of Charlemagne's best commanders.

The chanson states that the battle was seven years long and that it was fought against the Muslim Saracen tribe. Charlemagne is described as an old man with a white flowing beard. The portrayal of the people and events described in *La Chanson de Roland* do not give an accurate version of the story of the Battle of Roncesvalles.

Einhard's *Vita Caroli,* as well as other records that were made during Charlemagne's reign, give more reliable evidence about the battle. Nonetheless, the chanson is an interesting source that shows how later medieval people wanted to think about Charlemagne and what stories they wanted to tell of their history.

Basques were particularly brutal since Charlemagne had attacked Pamplona, their main city.

In spite of the defeat by the Basques, Charlemagne did bring the area along the Spanish border (the Marches) into his kingdom. He also

This example of Viking art dates from the ninth century. It was found on the island of Gotland in Sweden. The carved stone illustrates dead Vikings who are making their last voyage to Valhalla. Valhalla is where Vikings believed they traveled to in the afterlife. It was thought to be a place that was similar to heaven.

overcame the Slavs and Avars. They were both tribes from eastern Europe who were raiding the borders of his empire. Toward the end of his reign, Charlemagne successfully defended his empire against the Viking tribe from the far north of Europe (Scandinavia) when other rulers were failing against them. Charlemagne had ended most of his war campaigns by the time he was sixty-three. This was in the thirty-fourth year of his reign. Then he concentrated on governing his enormous empire.

CHARLEMAGNE BECOMES EMPEROR

Charlemagne generally kept good relations with many other leaders, including the Muslim rulers. He and other Frankish leaders thought of the Byzantine emperors as the most important rulers in Europe. Even though the Byzantine rulers were suspicious of the Franks, Charlemagne was on good terms with them.

In the year 797, Irene, who was acting as regent for her young son, Emperor Constantine VI, became the Byzantine empress after she and some powerful Byzantine nobles had Constantine removed from power. Because Roman law stated that women could not be rulers, the pope was not pleased by the way Irene had become ruler. This is one reason why the pope decided to make Charlemagne an emperor.

In the year 799, Pope Leo III was attacked by local leaders in Rome. The pope had to flee to Charlemagne and ask for help. Charlemagne and his army ended the rebellion and made sure the pope was safe and back in control of Rome. The following year, Charlemagne came to see the pope on Christmas Day. According to the *Vita Caroli*, when

Charlemagne went to greet Pope Leo, the pope suddenly placed a crown on Charlemagne's head and gave him the ancient Roman title of Imperator Augustus, or "Noble Emperor." Einhard wrote that this event took Charlemagne by surprise. He also said that if Charlemagne had known this was going to happen, he would not have visited the pope. However, it is not truly known whether Charlemagne actually knew about the coronation. Regardless, the result was that Charlemagne was made the most powerful ruler in Europe.

A CHRISTIAN EMPEROR

Charlemagne, who was a faithful Catholic Christian, wanted his empire to follow Catholic Christianity. He supported priests and churches in their attempts to convert people to Christianity. Like the previous Frankish kings, Charlemagne also supported the pope in Rome and often sent him expensive gifts and money. He also made many donations of relics, gold, silver, and clothes for priests who ran the churches.

Charlemagne made a law requiring that his people pay a special tax. This tax, called a tithe, was paid to the local church because he did not think that priests should do another job to earn money. The money was also used to help repair and rebuild churches.

Meanwhile, Muslim rulers in Spain allowed Christians to worship and have churches in their lands. However, the Christians in Muslim kingdoms had to follow special laws. For example, they were not allowed to preach their religion to Muslims. Also, if any Muslim was found to have been baptized, the punishment was death. During Charlemagne's time, Christianity did not spread as much in southern Europe as it did in northern Europe. This was because people pre-ferred to live as Muslims than to die as Christians. However, some people felt so strongly about being Christian that they were willing to die for their religion. These people became known as martyrs.

In Charlemagne's empire, churches were run by priests. The cathedrals (the large churches in the major cities of the empire) were run by bishops and archbishops. Bishops were very powerful, and some were the leaders of the cities they lived in.

Charlemagne himself was a very pious Catholic. As Einhard noted in the *Vita Caroli*, "He was a con-stant worshipper at this church as long as his health permitted, going morning and evening, even after nightfall." In church, Charlemagne enjoyed singing and chanting sacred Christian songs. He thought it was important for these songs to be sung in the same style as they were in the churches in Rome and the rest of Italy. He also wanted the Frankish churches to adopt the same ceremonies as the Catholic churches of Italy. According to Notker the Stammerer, the emperor created a songbook with instructions on how the songs should be sung. This was used long after Charlemagne's time.

CHARLEMAGNE'S CHURCH

During Charlemagne's reign, many churches, monasteries, and palaces were built and repaired. Charlemagne wanted to make sure that all his Christian subjects had good churches to go to and that the priests were well taken care of. His most important building project was his palace and church in his hometown of Aachen. He wanted these buildings to be as grand as those of the Byzantine Empire.

The most well-known Byzantine building was created by Emperor Justinian I between the years 532 and 537. It was called Hagia Sophia, which is Greek for the "Church of the Holy Wisdom." It was built in the style of a basilica with a massive dome and high arches. The interior was decorated with art depicting saints and scenes from Bible stories.

Charlemagne's palace and church were built between the years 790 and 805. The architecture incorporated many of the styles the Byzantines used

This is a photo of the interior of the Hagia Sophia in Constantinople (Istanbul). Saint Sophia was the patron saint of wisdom. This great church was built between 532 and 537 by Isidoros and Anthemios. Anthemios, who was born in the ancient city of Tralles in Asia Minor (modern-day Turkey), was a scientist and architect. Isidoros, an architect, engineer, and scholar, was born in Miletus (modern-day Turkey). After serving as a mosque for 400 years, the Hagia Sophia was turned into a museum in 1934.

in their basilicas, such as large domes and arches. The church was actually part of the palace itself and was not a separate building. This was for Charlemagne and his family and court to worship in. The church was dedicated to the Virgin Mary and was consecrated (made a holy place) in the year 805. In later years, it was made into a larger cathedral, much of which still stands. Charlemagne is said to have collected sacred relics for his church. Medieval churches that housed saints' relics were more likely to be visited by pilgrims.

PILGRIMS

Christians went on pilgrimages to visit the shrines of saints and to see the land where Jesus lived and died (the Holy Land). They hoped their journey would bring them closer to God and Jesus. Some hoped they would be cured of a disease or injury. They believed that the relics in the saint's shrine had magical powers that could grant a wish or have healing powers. Their journeys were often dangerous because the pilgrims could be caught in a battle or robbed. Bad weather could also cause problems, especially if they were traveling at sea. Poor pilgrims walked by foot, sometimes for months. Wealthier pilgrims could

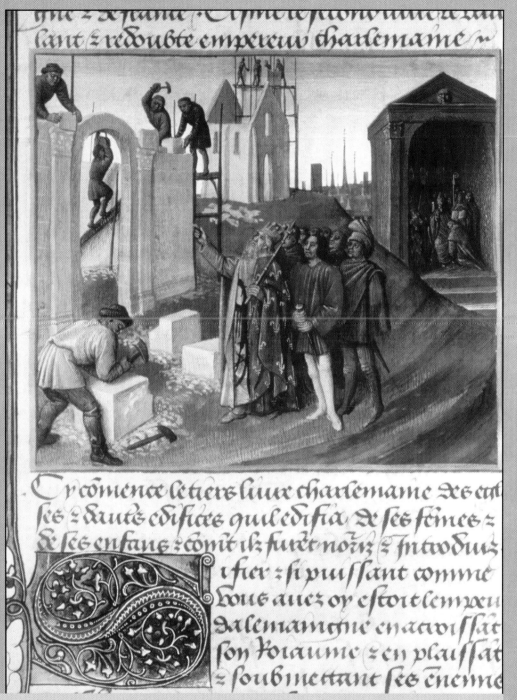

This image is from an illuminated manuscript called *Les Grandes Chroniques de France* (The Great Chronicles of France). It shows Charlemagne overseeing the building of his palace and church at Aachen, which later became a cathedral. In the background, Charlemagne is seen with his son Louis.

afford to buy horses. Charlemagne was worried about the safety of the pilgrims. He tried hard to be friendly with the Muslim leaders who ruled the lands European pilgrims had to go through on their way to the Holy Land.

Charlemagne also had a hospital built for pilgrims from his empire who traveled to St. Peter's Church in Rome (where the pope lived and worshipped). Medieval hospitals were places where pilgrims could rest, get food, and seek medical treatment if they were sick. They were usually run by the church. Charlemagne's hospital in Rome was called the Schola Francorum. He also helped Christians who did not live in his empire. In the *Vita Caroli*, Einhard wrote:

> When [Charlemagne] discovered that there were Christians living in poverty in Syria, Egypt, and Africa, at Jerusalem, Alexandria, and Carthage, he had compassion on their wants, and used to send money over the seas to them.

This kind of charity is called giving alms. Charlemagne felt passionately about the Christian subjects in his empire and those who lived abroad— rich and poor alike. He offered help and gave money

MONKS AND MONASTERIES

The word "monk" comes from the Greek *mono*, which means "single" or "alone." Early monks sometimes lived in the middle of nowhere, where they had no contact with other people. In the fifth century, Saint Benedict was the first monk to write rules for the way monks should live and behave. These rules (collectively called the Benedictine rule) dictated when monks should pray, how to pray, and what kind of work they should do to lead a holy life. All monks were supposed to perform manual labor such as farming, making beer and wine, or copying manuscripts. They wrote and copied manuscripts in the scriptorium (from the Latin word meaning "to write," *scribere*). The community of monks was led by an abbot. Nuns were female monks who lived in monasteries called nunneries. These were communities of women who also followed the Benedictine rule. Like the male monks, nuns farmed the land.

Although the life of a monk was meant to be simple and strict, by Charlemagne's time, being a monk could be very comfortable. Many monasteries were not taking the Benedictine rule seriously. They were protected by the emperor, and they did not have to fight in wars like other people. Often, the children of powerful noble families became monks in monasteries that their parents had set up on the family lands. Some children became monks when they were just five years old. Starting, or founding, a monastery could increase a family's status.

This image of the evangelist Matthew is from a Carolingian illuminated manuscript page that was written in the scriptorium of Charlemagne. It dates from the end of the eighth century. The manuscript page is most likely from Matthew's gospel in the New Testament. The four gospels are Matthew, Mark, Luke, and John.

to priests and pilgrims whenever he encountered them. Pilgrims also visited monasteries that housed saints' relics. Monks and monasteries were an important part of Charlemagne's empire. Monks helped spread the Christian faith throughout Charlemagne's empire. They played a significant role in converting people from pagan religions.

PAGANS

Even though Christianity was spreading in Europe during Charlemagne's reign, there were still many different followers of pagan religions. The Saxons of northeastern Germany were known as heathens (meaning "people of the heath or countryside") who worshipped gods such as Thor, Odin, and Freyja. They had their own temples and ceremonies. Many pagan ceremonies continued to be performed even after the heathens converted to Christianity. An example of such a ceremony is a German rain ritual, which was performed during times of drought.

JEWS AND MUSLIMS

Jews mainly lived in the cities of Charlemagne's empire. Many worked as merchants and business-people. Charlemagne allowed them to worship in their temples (synagogues), but they were not allowed to own land or have Christian laborers working for them. As well, they were not allowed to preach their religion to Christians. In the cities, Jews, Christians, Muslims, and pagans mixed together and did business together. There were not many Muslims living in Charlemagne's empire. However, there were many Muslim traders and merchants who brought exotic goods from Asia, Africa, and the Middle East to trade with people in the empire. Muslims also went on pilgrimages. They went to the holy city of Mecca, where the prophet Muhammad started the religion of Islam.

RUNNING AN EMPIRE

1 2 3 4 5 6 7

CHAPTER 5

As Charlemagne's empire grew, it became important to develop better methods of governing and keeping control of what was going on. Charlemagne took a personal interest in how his empire was run. He listened closely to his representatives, many of whom had traveled across the empire to bring him news from the Frankish nobles. He oversaw the building of palaces, churches, and roads. As well, he built bridges across large rivers such as the Rhine and Danube. Charlemagne did this so that his messengers and armies could travel across the empire more effectively.

Monks such as Einhard played an important role in helping to run Charlemagne's empire. Many royal officials were monks because they were some of the few people who could read and write. Monks at the

In this illustration from *Les Grandes Chroniques de France* ("The Great Chronicles of France"), Charlemagne is seen with his ambassadors *(top)*. Charlemagne would send people to the provinces of his empire so that they could report back to him and let him know how things were going. The bottom scene depicts the coronation of Charlemagne on Christmas Day in the year 800.

royal court were responsible for writing records like the Imperial Annals (official royal records of events), law codes, and letters on behalf of Charlemagne. Because monks could read and had studied Roman law in the monastery school, they were able to read the law codes and help Charlemagne understand them.

LAW

To rule his empire successfully, Charlemagne combined the use of Roman law with the style of government used by the German tribes of Europe. Roman law had a long history and was familiar to most rulers in Europe (except the Muslim rulers). The Byzantine Empire and the pope followed Roman law.

These were ancient laws developed by the Roman Republic (509–27 BC) and later by the Roman emperors (27 BC–AD 476). In the middle of the sixth century, the Byzantine emperor Justinian I reformed the Roman laws by having them written down in an orderly way so they were easier to understand. This is the version that Charlemagne's government followed. Using Roman law was important to Charlemagne because this showed the other rulers of Europe that he was a sophisticated king

This illustration from *Les Grandes Chroniques de France* ("The Great Chronicles of France") shows Charlemagne and his vassals. A vassal is someone who owes loyalty and obedience to a superior lord. In this case, the vassals' tribes may have been conquered by Charlemagne. The illustration shows many different events in Charlemagne's life, including a baptism *(far right)*.

and emperor. However, local nobles and bishops often acted as judges in their own lands and sometimes followed their own local laws.

Twice a year, the most important nobles in Charlemagne's empire would gather at court to talk about what was going on and to make laws to better govern the empire. At meetings such as these, Charlemagne acted as the judge, especially in difficult or important court cases.

TRAVELING ACROSS THE EMPIRE

Frankish rulers were well known for traveling across their kingdoms in person in order to govern their lands. Charlemagne and his court were almost always traveling around the empire until the later years of his life when he mainly stayed in Aachen. When visiting the important places in his empire, Charlemagne would be seen by local leaders. This would remind them of the king's supremacy. The Imperial Annals recorded the journeys that Charlemagne made during his reign (768–814). He made most of these journeys while he was still waging wars, until around 800.

The main routes were well known to Charlemagne, and he was protected by his bodyguards and his army. It was important that the roads and bridges along these routes were well maintained. Charlemagne would have had difficulty ruling such a large empire if he was not able to get to places quickly. Also, local Frankish leaders would have taken it as a sign that Charlemagne was a bad ruler if he did not visit their regions of the empire.

In the age before cars, people traveled over land by foot or by horse. The roads were not very smooth. In fact, sometimes they were impossible to pass through. Often, bridges were broken. In places where there were no bridges to cross the rivers, small boats or ferries were used. This made traveling around the empire very difficult. It also meant that it took a long time to travel to important places or move armies quickly during a war.

The most famous bridge Charlemagne had built was over the Rhine River at the city of Mainz in present-day Germany. Einhard writes in the *Vita Caroli* that the bridge was

> five hundred feet long, this being the width of the river, at that point. The bridge burned down just one year before Charlemagne's death. He planned to rebuild it in stone instead of wood, but his death followed so quickly that the bridge could not be restored in time.

During a journey to Rome, which was more than 800 miles (1,288 kilometers) long, Charlemagne would have had to cross the Alps and get through forests and boggy marshes. Because he was an ally of the pope, Charlemagne made several journeys to Rome. He made some of these journeys with his army to defend the pope when Rome or the Papal States were being attacked. It was important for Charlemagne to maintain close contact with the pope so that his empire kept the support of the Catholic Church. It is estimated that Charlemagne and his court traveled distances that would equal going around the world many times over.

MISSI DOMINICI

Charlemagne used messengers, called *missi dominici*, "messengers of the Lord," to get correspondence to other leaders. Exchanging messages with other rulers and with the Frankish nobles helped Charlemagne keep good relations with the European rulers. It also reminded them of his power. He could send gifts and invite foreign rulers and ambassadors to his palace at Aachen. Acting like a news service, the missi dominici brought Charlemagne reports of wars, the state of roads, and disputes between nobles. They could even alert Charlemagne if there were plots against his life. As well, the missi dominici took on the role of local judges who represented the king if there were court cases or disputes in the areas they traveled to.

One of their most important roles was to collect taxes. Taxes were the main source of income for Charlemagne's empire. The taxes paid for the wars; for the building of roads, bridges, and palaces; and for the royal officials. It would have taken a professional messenger more than one month to travel from the center of Charlemagne's empire to the edge of his empire in Spain.

This is an illustration from the Julian work calendar, which is a manual showing high days and holy days for each month of the church calendar. The calendar was probably written for young monks around 1020. This is the illustration for December. Pictured are peasants who are winnowing wheat (separating the chaff from the grain) and carrying away their harvest in finely woven baskets. Although these workers are Saxon, the Franks and other tribes did similar work.

Charlemagne had divided his empire into small units called counties and hundreds. These were ruled by nobles. The nobles also collected taxes from the peasants and serfs who worked on their land. In turn, the nobles gave some of the taxes to the missi dominici. Royal records kept an account of how much each hundred and county had paid. In the early Middle Ages, most of the taxes were paid by barter. For example, livestock (cows, sheep, pigs, and chickens) and wheat and other grains were commonly given as taxes.

THE RENAISSANCE OF CHARLEMAGNE'S REIGN

CHAPTER 6

From the year 800 on, Charlemagne fought in fewer wars. Because of this, he had more time to establish a strong system of government to rule his vast empire. Charlemagne ruled over most of western Europe and successfully kept the peace in his empire until his death in 814. This was also the period in which western Europe enjoyed a renaissance.

During this renaissance, learning and education spread across the empire as Charlemagne ordered schools to be opened. Many people, mostly monks, were writing and copying manuscripts more than anyone had in Europe since the fall of the Roman Empire in 476. People enjoyed living in more peaceful times, and merchants and businesspeople prospered in Charlemagne's empire. As well, churches and other public buildings were being built.

This is a photograph of the interior of Charlemagne's chapel. The chapel was constructed to serve as the imperial church and is now part of the Aachen Cathedral. The cathedral is a fine example of Carolingian architecture and one of the most important cultural monuments in Europe. It was built between 790 and 805. The design was inspired by the churches in the eastern Roman Empire. The cathedral was the first German monument to be admitted to the World Heritage List of UNESCO (United Nations Educational, Scientific and Cultural Organization) in 1978.

AACHEN BECOMES CHARLEMAGNE'S CAPITAL

One of the highlights of Charlemagne's renaissance was his magnificent palace at Aachen. Any visitor would be amazed at the size and richness of it. Every brick and tile was laid by hand. Odo of Metz was in charge of building the palace and its church between 790 and 805. Skilled artisans, probably from the

Byzantine Empire, were brought in to create beautiful decorations in gold, jewels, and mosaics. The mosaics were made from tiny tiles, which are called tesserae. Each tile was cut by hand and then painted. The palace and church were partly made from ancient marble that was discarded from Roman buildings in the cities of Rome and Ravenna. Large bronze doors were specially made for the palace. Lighting was provided by gold and silver lamps. These would have been hung from the walls and ceilings. Animal fat or oil would have been used as the fuel for the lamps.

The palace at Aachen was Charlemagne's main home. It was also where his government offices were. It was here that he planned wars and consulted with his advisers and nobles. The palace itself was like a small city. It housed Charlemagne's royal officers, court, and servants. The palace had large stores of food and wine for people to eat and drink. Most of this food and drink came from the royal estates in the Frankish kingdom that Charlemagne owned. The palace had a swimming pool, library, and weapons store. Charlemagne even created a school there.

Charlemagne's throne was carved out of a single piece of marble in the style of the thrones of the ancient Roman emperors. While sitting upon it,

This is Charlemagne's throne in Palatine Chapel, which is part of the cathedral at Aachen. An element of Carolingian architecture is the chapel's circular structure, which is unlike the rectangular design of many Roman-style churches. The throne, which is very simple, is only a little bit larger than a normal-sized chair. It is made from marble and wood.

Charlemagne towered above the members of his court and royal household. This was a reminder to his subjects that Charlemagne was the most important person in the kingdom. When he died, Charlemagne was buried with his throne.

THE PALACE SCHOOL

Charlemagne was very interested in learning new things, and he wanted his people to be educated too.

In the year 781, Charlemagne met a Saxon monk from Britain named Alcuin Albinus. Alcuin came to Charlemagne's court because he had heard that the king was looking for educated people to teach at his school. Charlemagne was so impressed by Alcuin that he wanted him to stay. Starting in 786, Alcuin ran the Palace School. Einhard said that Alcuin was "the most learned man anywhere to be found." Einhard was a teacher as well as a student at the school.

Alcuin's first student was Charlemagne. According to the *Vita Caroli*,

> Charlemagne received Alcuin with great kindness and kept him close at his side as long as he lived, except on the frequent occasions when he set out with his armies on mighty wars. The Emperor went so far as to have himself called Alcuin's pupil, and to call Alcuin his master.

Alcuin taught Charlemagne how to debate and speak in public. These were very important skills for a ruler. He also taught Charlemagne arithmetic, how to study the movement of the stars, and how to read and write. As well, they studied the Bible together.

Because there were few schoolbooks in Charlemagne's empire, Alcuin had to write them himself. According to the *Vita Caroli*, Charlemagne kept writing tablets and notebooks under his pillow so that in his spare time he could practice how to write. However, because Charlemagne started learning how to write at an old age, he was unable to write properly, even though he tried very hard. Peter the Deacon (who was from the monastery in Pisa, Italy) taught Charlemagne grammar and how to read and speak Latin and Greek.

The other students of the Palace School were Charlemagne's family, including his fourth wife, Liutgard, and his daughter Gisela. During his education, Charlemagne wrote a book about German grammar. He also collected old German poetry. Charlemagne was very interested in his own culture. He also liked to learn about medicine and music, and these subjects were taught at the school.

Charlemagne was shocked that so many of the churchmen could not read or write. He wondered how they understood and were able to speak about the teachings of the Bible to their congregations. In the year 787, Charlemagne made a royal order to the bishops and abbots. He demanded that they open schools in his empire so that others could be taught the things he was learning at the Palace School. The people who went to the schools were

ALCUIN'S VULGATE BIBLE

Charlemagne wanted a new version of the Bible to be written for his churches (at the time, the Catholic Church used many different versions). He thought it was important for all churches to read from the same Bible. Having a standard version would also help with his other reforms of church songs and ceremonies. Alcuin, Charlemagne's teacher, was one of the most knowledgeable people in Europe in terms of the Bible. He studied different versions that existed in many languages, including Latin and Greek. During his life, Alcuin worked on revising the Latin versions of the Bible into one standard version that could be used across Western Europe. This version has become known by many Catholics and historians as Alcuin's Vulgate Bible.

mainly monks and churchmen. They learned how to read and write, and they studied religion, philosophy, and science. At the time, schooling was usually for boys and adult men.

When Charlemagne had ordered Theodulf, the bishop of Orleans in France, to set up schools in all his lands, the bishop said the priests were not allowed to charge fees. However, it is not really known if this practice was followed. In the year 789, Charlemagne gave another royal order. This one stated that schools should teach serfs as well as free men. However, most of the children of serfs and peasants were expected to work in the fields and help their parents earn money for the family. Because of this, they were not able to attend. Some serfs who wanted to become free from working on a noble's lands all their lives might have joined a school to become monks.

WRITING AND BOOKS

Advances in writing were an important aspect of the renaissance that took place during Charlemagne's reign. As printing had not been invented at the time, documents were handwritten. Monks wrote and copied most of the documents historians have from the early Middle Ages. In fact, if monks hadn't copied and written manuscripts, historians would have very little information about ancient and early medieval times and people—including Charlemagne.

Most of the manuscripts were written and copied in the scriptoria (writing rooms) of monasteries. Many students in the monastery schools learned to write by copying other manuscripts. The monks mainly copied the Bible and the ancient

LEARNING

The Arabs preserved much of the classical learning of the ancient Greeks and Romans that is still important to European people. They also collected knowledge from the Persians, Indians, and Byzantines and combined this with their own learning in science and mathematics. In the year 780, the Arabs introduced algebra to Europe. In 789, Charlemagne ordered that the foot be the standard unit of measurement. Standard measurements were used to make accurate plans for the construction of bridges, ships, and buildings.

The schools in Charlemagne's empire taught what is known as the seven liberal arts. These included reading and writing in Latin and studying the Bible and the classical texts, as well as mathematics, astronomy, and music. Much of this knowledge came from the Arabs and the Byzantines.

There were few teachers like Alcuin and Peter the Deacon in the Frankish empire. Because of this, many teachers from the kingdoms in Britain, Ireland, and Italy came to teach in the Palace School and the other schools. Books were also brought over from these places. The schools created during Charlemagne's time would become the basis for the European universities that would emerge in the thirteenth century. The first universities were in Italy.

classical texts. The Bible and other books were very expensive in early medieval times because they took so long to copy. Most of these manuscripts were copied into Latin, because this was the official language of the empire. Writing and copying manu-scripts was a time-consuming and difficult job. The writer had to find any mistakes in the manuscript he was copying and be sure not to repeat them. The scriptoria were often cold and damp, and they only had candles and flame torches for light.

Book pages were made from parchment, which is sheep's skin. For writing tools, monks used quills made from large feathers that were dipped in pots of ink. Some books were illuminated with pictures of people and scenes of farming or hunting. Precious stones like lapis lazuli, which is a very deep blue color, were ground down to make paint for the illu-minations. Gold was also used. The book covers of luxury books were often made of ivory or were studded with precious jewels.

CAROLINGIAN MINUSCULE

Before Charlemagne's reign, all words in sentences were written in uppercase (capital) letters, and there were no spaces between words or any commas or periods. However, during Charlemagne's time, a new script called the Carolingian minuscule was invented. This script is the one that modern English writing is based on. Carolingian minuscule had spaces between words, upper- and lowercase letters, and punctuation such as commas and periods.

However, it would still be difficult to read today because medieval handwriting is different from modern handwriting.

This page from an illuminated manuscript shows an example of Carolingian minuscule, a new script that was developed during Charlemagne's reign. From the eighth to the twelfth century, this script was used to produce classical texts, religious books, and educational materials. After the Gothic period, the script was no longer used.

These expensive items were usually purchased by churches or cathedrals that wanted a grand copy of the Bible. Wealthy nobles also bought books, but since many of them could not read, these purchases were made as an attempt to show off their importance and wealth. In effect, because few people could read and books were luxury items, there was not a great demand for them.

LIVING AND WORKING IN THE COUNTRYSIDE

Most of the ordinary people in Charlemagne's empire lived in the countryside and worked on farms. The renaissance did not have a great impact on these peasants since the majority could not read and would not have been able to afford books. Some peasants owned small plots of land upon which they would grow food such as vegetables and beans. They would also keep their animals on the land.

Aside from the peasants, there were serfs (peasant slaves) who had to work on the land of a noble for life. They needed special permission from the noble in order to leave. Many serfs worked and lived in the same place all their lives. Peasants and serfs who worked on farms were important to the empire because they produced most of the food for both

This is an example of an illuminated manuscript that was copied onto parchment paper. Before monks or medieval scribes began to write out a manuscript, they had to decide if they were going to use paper or parchment. Though paper was cheaper and lighter, parchment was thought to be stronger and was easier to write on. The most beautiful and elaborate manuscripts were always done on parchment, because they would last longer.

ordinary people and the royal household. Charlemagne was interested in the way people farmed and what they traded. He asked for regular records, or an inventory, of the activities on his royal estates.

According to one inventory from about 800, Charlemagne kept a royal estate at Asnapium. The exact location of Asnapium is unknown, but it was likely to have been in western Germany or eastern France.

The royal estate had cows, pigs, sheep, goats, chickens, and peacocks. Wheat, oats, and barley were grown on the land for making bread and beer. There were apple and peach trees and a vegetable garden planted with garlic, onions, cabbage, and herbs such as sage. Farmers also lived on the estate and grew the crops. Workers who lived there would make bread and beer. Meanwhile, dairy workers made cheese and butter from the milk. Also living on the land were chefs who would do the cooking.

Charlemagne created rules for the workers as well as rules for how they should be cared for by their managers on the royal estates. For example, one rule (from Aquitaine) declared that the women who worked in the weaving workshop had to be provided with all the equipment they needed to do their job properly. The rule also stated that they needed to have a warm place to stay. It was up to stewards (the king's agents on the royal estates) to make sure these rules were followed. The stewards were allowed to act as judges if there was a disagreement or quarrel between the workers. They also had to make sure the people worked hard.

TRADE AND BUSINESS IN TOWNS

In addition to farming, trade was extremely important for Charlemagne's empire since merchants paid taxes as well. Merchants and artisans lived in towns and cities. This is where most of the important

This is a sixteenth-century map of Aachen, the center of Charlemagne's empire. Aachen was known as the "Rome of the north" when Charlemagne made it the center of his large European empire. Aachen lies in a valley and is surrounded by woods. There are many natural springs in the area.

trade and business took place. Before Charlemagne, merchants and businesspeople in Europe used many different currencies of coins with different amounts of silver and gold in them. The weight of gold or silver in a coin determined its value. This made trade and collecting taxes difficult. To simplify things, Charlemagne started minting his own coins that could be used throughout the empire. He created silver pennies that all had the same amount of silver in them and were the exact same size.

Merchants in Charlemagne's empire traded with British merchants over the North Sea and with Byzantine and Arab traders in southern Europe. They sold and exchanged their wares in markets throughout the empire. Charlemagne's government controlled the big markets in the cities. Charlemagne encouraged Frankish merchants to make deals with other merchants so that all sorts of different goods were brought into the empire. The Franks were very good at metalwork and they made excellent swords and knives that were mainly sold to merchants in northern Europe. They were also good at making things out of glass and clay. Some of these goods have survived and are currently kept in museums.

CHARLEMAGNE'S LEGACY

CHAPTER 7

The last years of Charlemagne's reign were becoming difficult as more tribes in Europe were attacking his empire. Charlemagne realized that it was becoming impossible for there to be only one ruler. Because of this, he made an order to divide the empire into three parts.

Each part was to be ruled by one of his three legitimate eldest sons: Charles, Pepin, and Louis. This was a traditional way for Frankish rulers to leave their property to their children. Charles was being made king of Frankland (the name of the central part of Charlemagne's empire). Pepin became king of the Lombards in northern Italy, and Louis became king of Aquitaine in Gaul. Regardless of the division, Charlemagne thought it was important that the three kingdoms were still seen as part of one Frankish Empire.

A NEW EMPEROR

Pepin and Charles both died suddenly in the years 810 and 811, and Charlemagne's plans to divide the empire were ruined. Charlemagne then thought it was important to make sure that his remaining son, Louis, was proclaimed as emperor so that when Charlemagne died it would be easier for Louis to rule alone.

Accordingly, in the year 813, Charlemagne and Louis had a special ceremony at Aachen Cathedral to name Louis as emperor. Just a year later, Charlemagne, who had been suffering from fevers and a lung disease called pleurisy, died at the age of seventy-two. In the *Vita Caroli*, Einhard writes that after Charlemagne

This is an illuminated manuscript illustration featuring Charlemagne as emperor, a scribe, and Charlemagne's son Pepin the Hunchback. Pepin was born before Charlemagne became king. Pepin could not become king and emperor even though he was Charlemagne's eldest child. This was because he was disabled, and the Franks believed that disabled men could not become leaders. Pepin's mother was Himiltrude but she was not known to have married Charlemagne.

died there was "great lamentation [sadness] of the entire population."

It is likely that the news of Charlemagne's death would have spread quickly across the empire. Many nobles would have come to Aachen to pay their respects to their emperor. For forty-seven years, Charlemagne had reigned over the largest empire in Europe since the Roman Empire. At his funeral, Charlemagne was placed sitting on his marble throne and lowered in a tomb in the church in his favorite palace at Aachen. There are no surviving descriptions of Charlemagne's funeral ceremony. The inscription on his tomb reads:

> Beneath this stone lies the body of Charles the Great, the Christian Emperor,
>
> who greatly expanded the kingdom of the Franks
>
> and reigned successfully for forty-seven years.
>
> He died when more than seventy years old in the eight hundred and fourteenth year of our Lord, in the seventh tax-year, on 28 January.

THE END OF CHARLEMAGNE'S EMPIRE

After Charlemagne died, Louis found it difficult to rule because he was being attacked by his own family. Louis was frightened for his life and was also worried about keeping the empire at peace. He sent many of his family members to monasteries so they could not rebel against him. However, this did not stop the family wars. Louis died in the year 840. In 843, the empire was once again divided—this time among Louis's three sons. The Treaty of Verdun was signed to seal the division.

Louis's eldest son, Lothair, was made emperor of Frankland, but his two brothers, Louis the German and Charles the Bald, were just kings. Louis and Charles were jealous of Lothair's power and did not want to be less powerful rulers. As a result, a civil war broke out in Charlemagne's old empire. For more than thirty years, the Frankish kings continued to fight against each other. While they were doing this, the empire fell apart and powerful noble families took control of much of it. None of Charlemagne's successors managed to reunite the Frankish Empire. By the end of the tenth century, the line of Carolingian rulers had ended.

SAINT CHARLEMAGNE

Two hundred years after Charlemagne's death, Otto III was emperor. It was coming up to the end of the first millennium (the year 1000). Charlemagne was Otto III's hero, and he wanted to celebrate the millennium by opening Charlemagne's tomb at Aachen Cathedral. Otto found that Charlemagne was sitting on his marble throne, wearing his robes and crown, and holding the Bible on his lap. It was as though he were still emperor. Otto marveled that the emperor's body had not rotted. He even noticed that the dead emperor's fingernails had grown. It is said that Otto trimmed Charlemagne's nails and then reburied him.

From this time on, people started to believe that, though he was dead, Charlemagne had special powers just like other saints and their relics. Many people came to visit his tomb while on pilgrimage. In the year 1165, during the reign of Emperor Frederick Barbarossa, Charlemagne was made a saint but he was never officially recognized as a Catholic saint by the pope in Rome because the "antipope" Paschal performed the canonization (saint-making ceremony). During the twelfth century, German emperors such as Frederick Barbarossa wanted a say in who should become the pope. When they did not get their choice, they often chose another man anyway. This meant there were sometimes two men proclaiming themselves as pope. One of these was known as the antipope.

Charlemagne's relics (his bones) were later placed in reliquaries. These are special caskets for the bones of saints that pilgrims could see and touch. One

reliquary is in the shape of a giant golden arm that contains Charlemagne's actual arm bones. The golden bust of Charlemagne contains his skull. When pilgrims come to visit Charlemagne's shrine at Aachen, they can kiss the skull through a little door at the back for good luck or to be healed. Kissing relics is also a sign of respect. It became a custom for Charlemagne's relics to be brought out every seven years.

This is a full-length statue of Charlemagne from a church in Dortmund. It dates from the fifteenth century. He is wearing armor and a crown and carrying the symbols of kingship—the orb in his left hand and the scepter in his right. The orb symbolizes his rule on earth and is surmounted by a cross to indicate that he is the anointed representative of God. The scepter is the symbol of his authority and power over the subjects of his kingdom and empire.

Thousands of pilgrims have visited Charlemagne's shrine at Aachen since medieval times. This custom still carries on. The last time Charlemagne's relics were brought out was in the year 2000.

TIMELINE

476   Fall of Rome. The last western Roman emperor is overthrown, indicating the end of the ancient Roman Empire in western Europe.

732   Battle of Poitiers in Gaul (France). Charles Martel, Charlemagne's grandfather, defeats the Muslim ruler Abd al-Rahman.

742   Birth of Charlemagne, possibly in Aachen.

751   Pepin the Short is elected king of the Franks and is anointed by Bishop Boniface.

753   Pope Stephen II travels to the Frankish kingdom to ask Pepin the Short for help in his war against the Lombards.

754   The pope anoints Pepin, Charlemagne, and Carloman as kings of the Franks.

768   Pepin the Short dies, and Charlemagne and Carloman become joint rulers of the Frankish kingdom.

771   Charlemagne becomes the sole king of the Franks when his brother, Carloman, dies.

772   Charlemagne orders the destruction of Irminsul, the sacred shrine of the Saxons.

774   Charlemagne defeats the Lombards and adds their kingdom to the Frankish Empire.

778   Battle of Roncesvalles in southern Gaul. Charlemagne's army is defeated by the Basque tribe.

781   Charlemagne meets Alcuin, a Saxon monk from England. He persuades Alcuin to come to the Palace School at Aachen to help teach Charlemagne reform the way the church was run.

782   Charlemagne orders the execution of 4,500 Saxons.

785	Widukind, a Saxon ruler, and his army convert to Christianity to make peace with Charlemagne and to end the Saxon wars.
787	Charlemagne orders bishops and abbots in the Frankish Empire to open schools.
790	Construction begins of Charlemagne's palace at Aachen.
800	Charlemagne is anointed emperor of the Franks by Pope Leo III at Rome.
805	Charlemagne has his palace church consecrated and dedicated to the Virgin Mary.
810–811	Death of Charles and Pepin, Charlemagne's sons.
813	Louis the Pious, Charlemagne's surviving son, is crowned as emperor of the Franks.
814	Charlemagne dies of fevers and infection of the lungs. He is buried in his palace church at Aachen.
830	Einhard, a Frankish monk and Charlemagne's friend, begins to write the *Vita Caroli* ("Life of Charlemagne").
843	Treaty of Verdun divides Charlemagne's empire forever.
About 1150	*The Song of Roland* is written about the Battle of Roncesvalles.
1165	Charlemagne is made a saint during the reign of Emperor Frederick Barbarossa.

GLOSSARY

alms   Charity given to the poor and needy, usually in the form of basic foods such as bread. Churches, monasteries, and hospitals, as well as wealthy families, gave alms to the poor.

annals   Medieval manuscripts that contain lists and descriptions of historic events such as wars. Usually the annals were written by monks who worked in the royal court. Charlemagne's annals were called the Imperial Annals.

anoint   To perform a sacred ceremony in order to baptize someone or make someone a king, priest, or emperor, usually by a Christian priest. During the ceremony, holy oil was traced on the person's face in the shape of a cross.

artisan   Someone who makes things for a living. For example, a blacksmith makes knives, swords, and horseshoes out of metal.

baptism   A holy ceremony performed by a priest on people who become Christian. Holy water is used during the ceremony.

basileus   The Greek word for emperor.

basilica   A style of church building used mainly in southern and eastern Europe, especially during the Byzantine Empire. These buildings had wide aisles and usually had a large dome over the area of the altar, which is the most holy part of a church.

Benedictine rule   The set of laws written by Saint Benedict for monks to follow. The rule told monks when to pray, what type of work to do, and how they should worship God.

bishop   An important priest who ran the cathedrals in large medieval cities. Bishops were often powerful leaders who could also be the local ruler of a city and its surrounding areas. Archbishops were more important and powerful than bishops. They ran the cathedrals in the most important cities of the empire.

boar   A type of wild pig that lives in forests.

caliph   An Arabic word for a Muslim ruler.

Carolingian   The ruling dynasty (family line) of the Franks that Charlemagne and his successors came from.

Carolingian minuscule   The style of writing developed during Charlemagne's reign.

chanson   The French word for "song."

Christendom   The kingdoms in Europe that were led by Christian rulers and whose people were mainly Christian.

chronicle   A medieval document, usually written by monks, about the history of cities or kingdoms, or the history of great leaders.

classical   Relating to the worlds and cultures of the ancient Greeks and Romans.

congregation   A group of worshippers who have gathered together in a church to pray and hear the priest's sermon.

consecration   A religious ceremony performed by a priest to make a new church a holy place and to give it a name.

county   A unit of land. Counties were smaller than kingdoms but bigger than hundreds. The county was usually run by a noble given the title of count and was appointed by the emperor.

court   The group of royal officials who help a king or emperor run his kingdom or empire. The court was often comprised of close family members and friends of the king or emperor, monks who would help write royal records such as the Imperial Annals, and army leaders. The court usually lived in the royal palace.

dynasty   A family line of rulers. Charlemagne was from the Carolingian dynasty.

emir   A king or chieftain; a term used by Muslim Arab and African rulers.

estate   Land belonging to a noble. Royal estates were owned by kings and emperors.

fasting   Not eating on certain holy days for religious reasons.

feast days   Special days in the year that are devoted to the celebration of a particular saint or important time in the Christian calendar.

foot   A unit of measurement that was made a common unit during Charlemagne's reign. Apparently, it was as long as the emperor's foot.

heathen   The name of pagans from northern Europe, such as the Saxons, meaning "people of the heath or countryside."

hundred   A unit of land used by Charlemagne to govern his empire. Many hundreds made up a county and were about the size of a small village or farm.

inventory   A survey of items that are part of an estate. It included buildings, workers such as farm laborers, animals, food, and furniture. Charlemagne ordered inventories of his royal estates so he knew what he owned and what activities were going on.

Irminsul   A sacred symbol of the heathens. It was also a sacred pillar that heathens used in their religious worship. Charlemagne destroyed the Irminsul of the Saxons at Marseburg in 772.

laypeople   People who are not members of the clergy, such as priests, monks, or nuns.

manuscript   A document usually written on parchment (dried and flattened sheep skin) with ink. Illuminated manuscripts contain many beautiful and colorful pictures painted with inks that are made from precious stones and natural dyes that are made from vegetables, wood, and sea creatures.

Marches   The area around the borders of two kingdoms. Charlemagne ruled over the Marches of Spain in the north of the country, at the border of Gaul (modern-day France).

martyr   Someone who is willing to die for the sake of his or her religion.

mercenary   A professional soldier who is paid to fight battles by nobles and kings in their armies.

missi dominici   Latin for "messengers of the lord." These were special messengers sent by Charlemagne to all the different counties and hundreds of his empire. They sent and received messages from local leaders, collected taxes, and made sure the law was being followed.

missionary   A religious person who travels to different lands trying to convert people to Christianity.

patriarch   The title of the most important bishop in the Byzantine Empire. The title was only used for the bishop of Constantinople and was similar to the pope in Rome. The patriarch crowned the Byzantine emperors.

peasant   Laborers, usually farmers, on a noble's estate or on a royal estate.

pilgrim   A person making a special journey to a religious place, such as a saint's shrine, or to major Christian centers like Rome and Jerusalem. Pilgrims followed certain routes, where they paid homage to churches and saints' shrines on the way to their destination.

pope   The title of the most important bishop in western Europe. The title was used only for the bishop of Rome whose role was similar to the patriarch of the Byzantine Empire. The pope crowned kings, queens, and emperors of western Europe.

relic   A sacred object, usually the bone or a piece of cloth from a holy person or a saint. Relics were believed to be powerful objects that could heal and grant wishes. Pilgrims would journey long distances to touch a relic. Charlemagne collected relics believed to be connected to Jesus, Mary, the saints, and ancient emperors such as Constantine.

renaissance   A time of big developments in art, writing, music, and architecture.

scriptorium   The Latin word for a writing room. Scriptoria were found in many monasteries where monks wrote and copied manuscripts.

serf   A peasant who is tied to the land of a noble for life. Serfs had to work the land and give some of the harvest to the noble in return for a place to stay. Serfs were like slaves. They could not stop working for the noble unless he or she got permission to be freed.

seven liberal arts   Medieval school subjects. These were put in two groups: the trivium was grammar (how to write), rhetoric (how to speak), and logic (how to think). The quadrivium was mathematics, arts, astronomy, and music. These were areas of knowledge the ancient Romans studied as well.

subjects   People who are ruled by a king, queen, or emperor.

tithe A special tax paid by laypeople to the church. It means "a tenth" and was meant to be one-tenth of someone's earnings or one-tenth of the harvest produced on a farm.

treasury A room in a palace, church, or cathedral where precious objects are kept.

venison The meat from a deer.

Vulgate A Bible written in common Latin, a language that most priests would understand and be able to translate for their congregations.

FOR MORE INFORMATION

WEB SITES

Due to the changing nature of Internet links, the Rosen Publishing Group, Inc., has developed an online list of Web sites related to the subject of this book. This site is updated regularly. Please use this link to access the list:

http://www.rosenlinks.com/lema/char

FOR FURTHER READING

Biel, Timothy L. *The Importance of Charlemagne.* San Diego: Lucent Books, 1997.

Hanawalt, Barbara A. *The Middle Ages: An Illustrated History.* Oxford, England: Oxford University Press Children's Books, 1999.

Langley, Andrew. *Eyewitness Medieval Life.* London: Dorling Kindersley, 2002.

Nicolle, David, and Martin Windrow. *Age of Charlemagne.* Oxford, England: Osprey, 1984.

Willard, Barbara. *Son of Charlemagne.* Bathgate, ND: Bethlehem Books, 1998.

BIBLIOGRAPHY

Amt, Emilie, ed. *Women's Lives in Medieval Europe.* London: Routledge, 1993.

Atlet, Xavier Barral I., and Lory Frankel, trans. *The Early Middle Ages from Late Antiquity to AD 1000.* Cologne, Germany: Taschen, 2002.

Catholic Encyclopedia. "Charlemagne." Retrieved July 15, 2003 (http://www. newadvent.org/cathen/03610c.htm).

Collins, Roger. *Charlemagne.* Basingstoke, England: Palgrave Macmillan, 1998.

Collins, Roger. *Early Medieval Europe 300–1000.* Basingstoke, England: Palgrave Macmillan, 1999.

Grant, Michael. *The Fall of the Roman Empire.* London: Phoenix Giant, 1997.

Halsall, Paul. "Asnapium: An Inventory of One of Charlemagne's Estates c. 800—Internet Medieval Sourcebook." Retrieved July 30, 2003 (http://www.fordham.edu/halsall/ source/800Asnapium.html).

Hamilton, Bernard. *Religion in the Medieval West.* London: Edward Arnold, 1986.

HistoryWorld. "Europe in the Time of Charlemagne." Retrieved July 15, 2003 (http://www. historyworld.net).

King, P. D. *Charlemagne: Translated Sources.* Kendal, England: P. D. King, 1987.

Kreis, Steven. "The History Guide: Lectures on Ancient and Medieval History." Retrieved July 23, 2003 (http://www.historyguide.org/ancient/ancient.html).

Loverance, Rowena. *Byzantium.* London: British Museum, 1988.

Matthews, John, and Bob Steward. *Warriors of Christendom.* London: Brockhampton Press, 1993.

Nelson, Lynn Harry. "The Song of Roland." Retrieved August 8, 2003 (http://www.ku.edu/kansas/ medieval/108/lectures/roland.html).

Nicholas, David. *The Growth of the Medieval City.* London: Longman, 1997.

Nicolle, David. *The Age of Charlemagne.* Oxford, England: Osprey, 1984.

Ohler, Norbert, and Caroline Hillier, trans. *The Medieval Traveller.* Woodbridge, England: Boydell Press, 1995.

The Online Medieval and Classical Library. "Song of Roland." Retrieved August 5, 2003 (http://sunsite. berkeley.edu/OMACL/Roland).

Parker, Geoffrey, ed. *The Times Compact Atlas of World History.* London: Times Books, 1995.

Riché, Pierre, and Jo Ann McNamara, trans. *Daily Life in the World of Charlemagne.* Philadelphia: University of Pennsylvania Press, 1978.

Price, Brian R. "Charlemagne the King: An [sic] biography from Will Durant's Story of Civilisation 1950." 2000. Retrieved July 30, 2003 (http://www.chronique.com/ Library/MedHistory/charlemagne.htm).

Thorpe, Lewis, trans. *Einhard and Notker the Stammerer: Two Lives of Charlemagne.* London: Penguin, 1969.

Thorpe, Lewis, trans. *Gregory of Tours: The History of the Franks.* London: Penguin, 1974.

Wickham, Chris. *Early Medieval Italy: Central Power and Local Society 400–1000.* Ann Arbor, MI: University of Michigan Press, 1989.

Wikipedia. "Holy Roman Empire." Retrieved July 27, 2003 (http://www.wikipedia.org/wiki/ Holy_Roman_Empire).

Winston, Richard. *Charlemagne.* London: Cassel, 1969.

INDEX

About the Author

Tehmina Bhote was born in 1978 and was brought up in London, England. She now lives in Southampton. She runs local history projects to increase access to collections from libraries, museums, and archives for the public. She is studying for a Ph.D. in early medieval Italian material culture and also teaches history to undergraduates at the University of Southampton.

CREDITS

Designer: Evelyn Horovicz
Editor: Annie Sommers
Photo Researcher: Elizabeth Loving